Floating and Sinking

Written by Sarah O'Neil
Photography by Michael Curtain

Some things float.
Some things sink.

What helps them
to float or to sink?

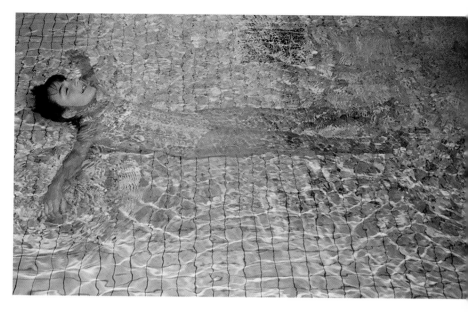

What is floating?

This apple is in the water.
It is floating.

What is sinking?

This potato is in the water.
It has sunk.

Some things float because of what they are made of.

This truck is plastic.
Plastic is light.
The plastic truck is floating.

Some things sink because of what they are made of.

This truck is metal.
Metal is heavy.
The metal truck has sunk.

Some things float
because of their shape.

This modeling clay
has been made into a boat.
It is floating.

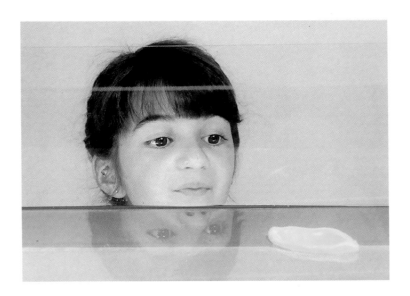

Some things sink
because of their shape.

This modeling clay has been
made into a ball.
It has sunk.

Some things float or sink
because of how they go
into the water.

Put a bowl flat on the water.
It will float.

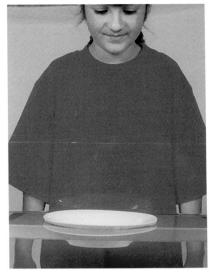

Put a bowl sideways
into the water.
It will sink.

People float and sink.

This girl is lying flat in the water.
She is floating.

This girl is upright in the water.
She is sinking.

People can float or sink because
of the way they move.

This girl is not moving
her arms or legs.
She is sinking.

This girl is moving
her arms and legs.
She is not sinking.

Find out if these things float or sink.